What is a Storm?

By Sophia Evans

Library For All Ltd.

Library For All is an Australian not for profit organisation with a mission to make knowledge accessible to all via an innovative digital library solution.
Visit us at libraryforall.org

What is a Storm?

First published 2021

Published by Library For All Ltd
Email: info@libraryforall.org
URL: libraryforall.org

This work is licensed under the Creative Commons Attribution-NonCommercial-NoDerivatives 4.0 International License. To view a copy of this license, visit http://creativecommons.org/licenses/by-nc-nd/4.0/.

This book was made possible by the generous support of the Education Cooperation Program and the following organisations.

  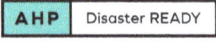

What is a Storm?
Evans, Sophia
ISBN: 978-1-922550-22-4
SKU01572

Images sourced from pixabay.com, wikimedia.org and maxpixel.net under a CCO license.

What is a Storm?

Weather

Weather is the temperature, rainfall, sunshine and cloudiness in an area at any one time.

Did you know?

There can be different types of weather in the same day.

Sometimes the weather is hot and rainy. Sometimes it is cold and cloudy.

Storms

A storm is a type of weather. In a storm there can be very strong winds, heavy rain, hail, thunder and lightning.

Storms can be very dangerous.

Storms can happen at any time. Some storms are small and some storms are big. If a storm is really bad you might need to evacuate.

Evacuate means you leave your home to go somewhere that is safer.

Did you know?

Rain

Inside a cloud there are tiny bits of water and ice. When the tiny water drops join together, they are too heavy to stay in the cloud. These water drops are called rain.

Rain can be light or heavy. In a storm there is heavy rain.

Heavy rain can cause flooding or landslides.

Hail

Hail is formed the same way as rain except that it becomes frozen when it's in the cloud. The little water and ice pieces stick together. These form bigger pieces that fall from the clouds.

Hail can be the size of a fist.

Hail is formed in clouds then falls to the ground. It can hit people, buildings and cars and cause damage.

Thunder and Lightning

Thunder and lightning happen at the same time. Sometimes when the tiny pieces of water and ice bump into each other in clouds, they create electricity. Lightning is the bright flash of electricity that can't stay in clouds. The sound of this electricity coming to the ground is called thunder.

When you clap your hands you trap air which is similar to the sound of thunder. When thunder happens in clouds, the air is trapped by other air and water droplets, not by giant hands.

Wind

Wind is air that is moving. Sometimes the air doesn't move very fast and it feels still. When wind moves very fast, it can become dangerous to be outside.

Strong winds can knock down trees or blow the roof off a house.

You can make your own wind using a fan or by waving your arms!

There are signs to tell when a storm is coming.

14

Know the signs

When a storm is coming, clouds get darker because they are full of rain. Sometimes you can smell rain before it happens. You might hear the sound of thunder rumbling. The wind might get stronger and sometimes it changes direction.

Make sure you stay safe when a storm is coming.

Be Prepared

A storm can happen at any time so it is important to know what to do. It is a good idea to have an emergency kit and a safety plan.

A safety plan

A safety plan is what your family decides to do if there is an emergency. It helps everyone know what to do and where to go. Each person can be in charge of doing something to keep everyone safe.

> Your job might be to tie up your boat, make sure your pets are safe or get the emergency kit.

An emergency kit

1

First aid kit including any medication you need

2

Tinned food and a can opener

3

Bottled water

4 Toiletries including toilet paper, toothpaste, soap, insect repellent and a mosquito net

Warm, dry clothing

6 Battery operated radio and batteries

Waterproof matches and a way to cook food

TAKE CARE OF YOURSELF

Stay safe

It's important to stay safe during and after a storm.

Stay inside until the storm has stopped.	Stay out of flood water.
Stay away from windows in case of hail.	Stay away from trees as they could fall over.

Can you collect the items from the emergency kit and get to safety?

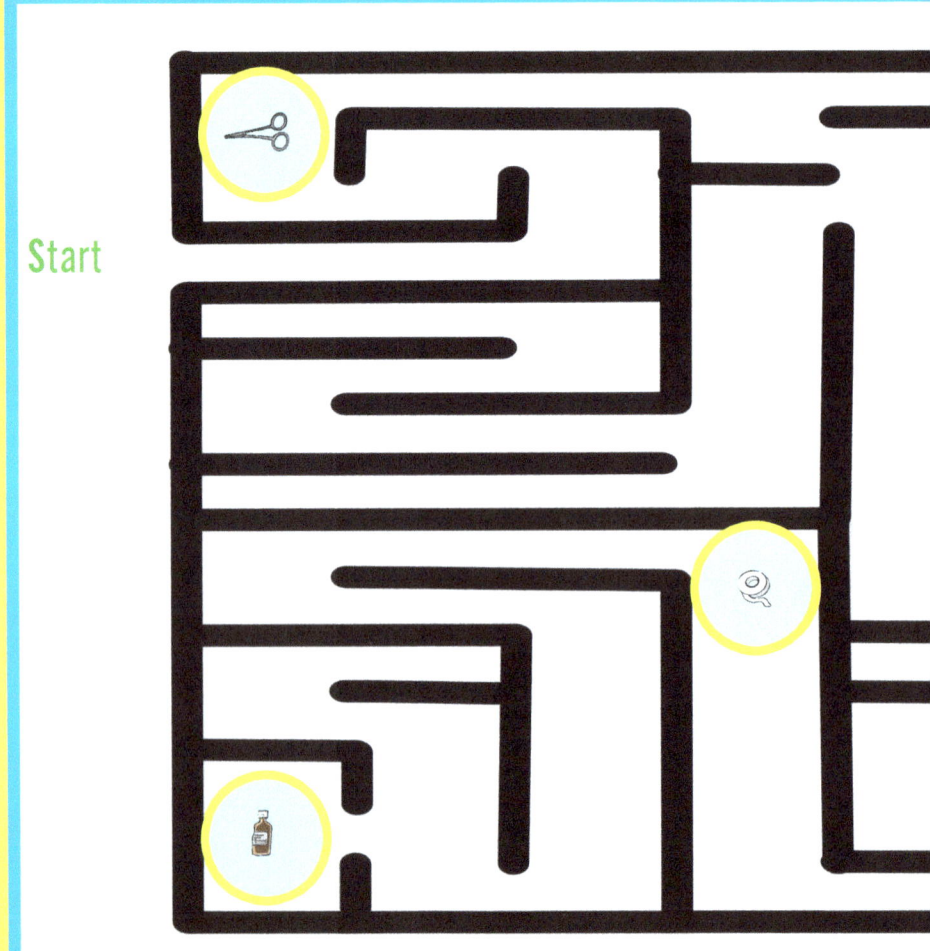

Emergency decision-making tree

Prior to the event of a tsunami, tropical cyclone, flooding, landslide or earthquake, speak with your family and teacher about your community's evacuation building or safe place.

Discuss how to respond to possible scenarios, and use the decision tree to help you decide the best course of action.

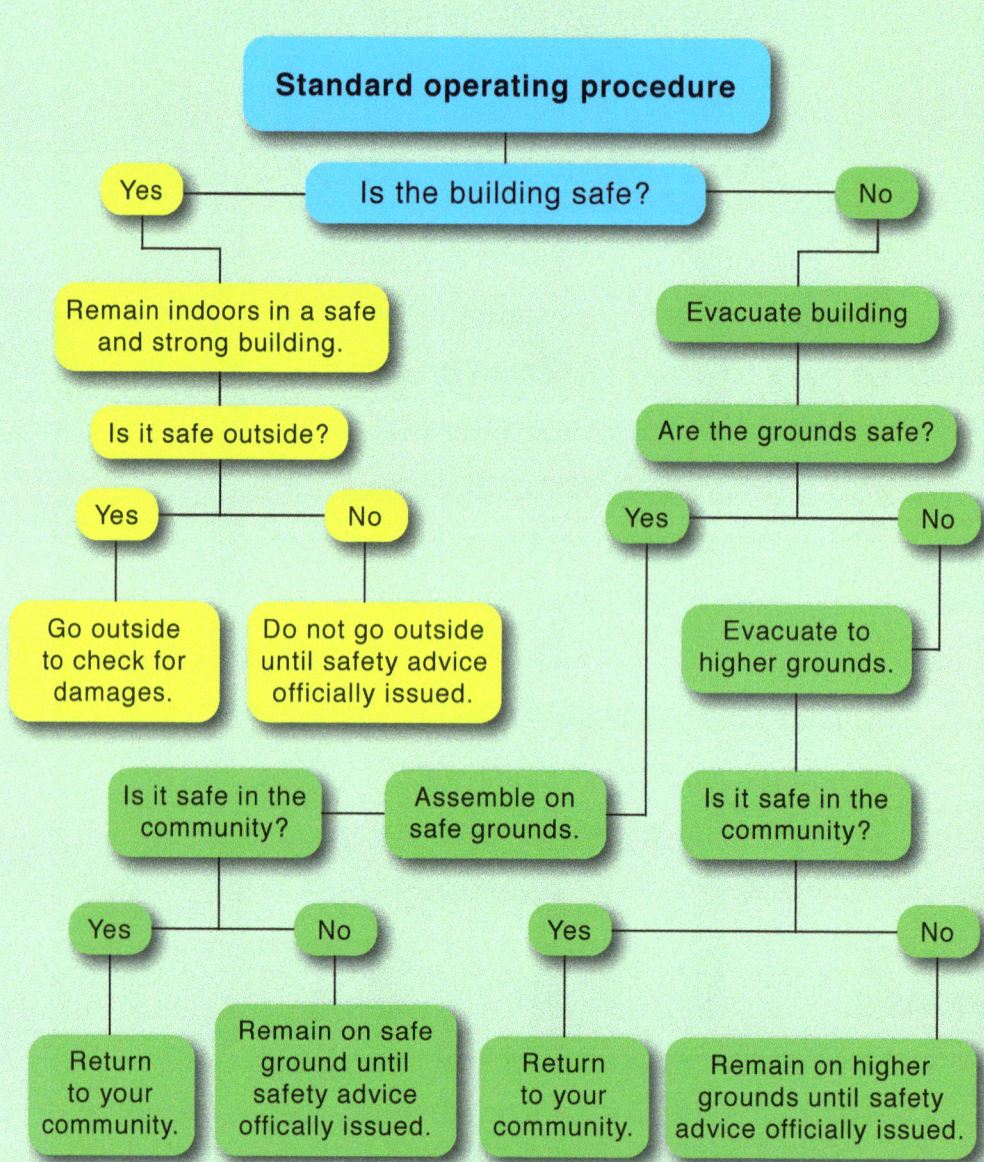

Supporting information

Emergency kit

Keep an emergency kit at home for your family.

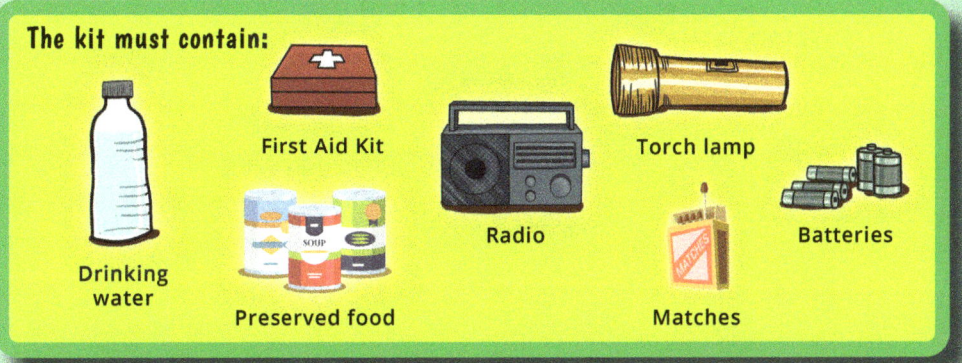

Use the kit only in case of emergency and replace anything that has been used.

Shelter-in-place

Earthquake:
- Identify safe places where you can protect your head and avoid heavy falling objects.
- Don't forget an earthquake can cause a tsunami.
- If you feel a strong earthquake, go quickly to higher ground, and listen to the radio for warnings.

Tropical cyclone:
- Open louvers on the side of the building, away from wind to reduce the pull force of the wind on the roof.
- Remain calm, stay indoors but clear of doors and windows.
- Remain in the strongest part of the building.

Do not go outside until safety advice is officially issued.

Evacuate building

Assist people with disability and visitors.
Take your emergency kit.
Evacuate to higher ground and move to a safe location.

Tsunami:
- Run to a safe place in high ground or at least 2 km inside the island.
- Wait for at least 2-3 hours after the first wave to return to the village.

Listen to the radio for further information or reach out to the emergency contacts.

You can use these questions to talk about this book with your family, friends and teachers.

What did you learn from this book?

Describe this book in one word. Funny? Scary? Colourful? Interesting?

How did this book make you feel when you finished reading it?

What was your favourite part of this book?

download our reader app
getlibraryforall.org

About the contributors

Library For All works with authors and illustrators from around the world to develop diverse, relevant, high quality stories for young readers. Visit libraryforall.org for the latest news on writers' workshop events, submission guidelines and other creative opportunities.

Did you enjoy this book?

We have hundreds more expertly curated original stories to choose from.

We work in partnership with authors, educators, cultural advisors, governments and NGOs to bring the joy of reading to children everywhere.

Did you know?

We create global impact in these fields by embracing the United Nations Sustainable Development Goals.

libraryforall.org

www.ingramcontent.com/pod-product-compliance
Lightning Source LLC
Chambersburg PA
CBHW040316050426
42452CB00018B/2867